Growing in Grace

Growing in Grace

Michael L. Sherer

C.S.S. Publishing Company, Inc.
Lima, Ohio

GROWING IN GRACE

Copyright © 1986 by
The C.S.S. Publishing Company, Inc.
Lima, Ohio

All rights reserved. No part of this publication may be reproduced, stored in a retrieval system, or transmitted in any form or by any means, electronic, mechanical, photocopying, recording, or otherwise, without the prior permission of the publisher. Inquiries should be addressed to: The C.S.S. Publishing Company, Inc., 628 South Main Street, Lima, Ohio 45804.

Library of Congress Cataloging-in-Publication Data

Sherer, Michael L.
    Growing in grace.

    Summary: Portrays appropriate Christian behavior by depicting young people dealing with such situations as drinking, premarital sex, and trying to understand parents. Includes discussion questions and suggestions for Bible readings.
    1. Youth—Religious life. [1. Christian life]
I. Title.
BV4515.2.S54   1986   248.8'3   85-28996
ISBN 0-89536-798-X

6816 / ISBN 0-89536-798-X   PRINTED IN U.S.A.

*Dedicated to my recently-confirmed young friends:
Wendy, Karlyn, Gary, Scott
Called by God to grow in grace each day*

Continue to strengthen them with the Holy Spirit,
and daily increase in them your gifts of grace:

the spirit of wisdom and understanding
the spirit of counsel and might
the spirit of knowledge and the fear of the Lord
the spirit of joy in your presence . . .

>From a prayer for those
affirming their baptism

Lutheran Book of Worship

Table of Contents

A Word to the Reader   11

1. The Sacred Stripe   13
   Coming alive to our baptism

2. One Out of Ten   21
   Responsible use of sexuality

3. A Sudden Sacrifice   28
   Forgiving when it isn't easy

4. A Miracle at One O'clock   33
   Sharing feelings with your parents

5. Easter Jones   38
   Death and new life

6. The Winner and Still Champion   44
   Dealing honestly with others

7. Something Old, Something New   51
   Discovering value in our heritage

8. Strange Parade   58
   Remembering God while on vacation

9. A Real Steal   65
   Stewardship and justice

10. Halloween With a Twist   72
    Repentance and forgiveness

11. A-Time in the Morning   78
    Building your prayer life

12. Christmas in Reverse   84
    Discovering the true meaning of the celebration

A Word to the Reader

When you were confirmed you promised God you would do everything you could to be faithful to him. But living in God's kingdom isn't always easy. Here are stories about twelve confirmed young people, some of whom may be a lot like you. In fact, as you read their stories, you may even feel as though some of the same things have already happened in your life.

Following each story there are three of four thought-provokers and ideas to get you to think about how you can use that story to make your life in God's family more successful. Every story also has some sort of tie to a story from Scripture. After you have read about Josh, Alex, Jon, Kim, Jennie and the others, you may want to find the Scripture story and see how it casts some extra light on what you've read. Why not use the Bible you used when you were in confirmation class?

Enjoy these stories. If you think they're good, and you would like to see some more, you might send a note to the publisher (the address is: C.S.S. Publishing Company, 628 S. Main Street, Lima, Ohio 45804).

And, if you have some friends whom you think would enjoy this book, consider passing it along to them when you are finished.

The Sacred Stripe

Sometimes you feel as though your baptism is something "long ago and far away." What difference does it make, really, that someone poured a little water on your head when you were too young to remember it? That's just what Josh Cornelius was wondering...

It was raining. Josh Cornelius first Thought he had only dreamed it. But when he awoke early that Saturday he realized it wasn't his imagination. Water was coming down the panes of the cabin windows in rivulets, chasing one another.

"Darn!" he muttered, just loud enough for Paul Weber, in the next bed, to hear.

Paul stirred, then stretched and opened his eyes. "What's the problem?" he asked, looking groggily at Josh.

"Just listen. Look," said Josh, pointing disgustedly toward the window.

Paul pulled down the zipper on his sleeping bag, swung his legs out and sat up on the side of the bed. "Oh, man. What a bummer," said Paul. A whole weekend trapped inside. Blast it. I thought we came on this retreat to have some fun."

"Looks like we thought wrong, buddy," Josh said, getting up and pulling on his jeans. "You know something? This could get to be real boring. Now we're stuck with Pastor Dave's ideas. He'll probably make us sit inside all day and read the Bible. Echhh."

Pastor Dave Wassermann was the youth pastor at Christ the Shepherd Church. He'd brought the dozen recently confirmed kids from the congregation up to camp this weekend. He had told them they were going to talk about "belonging to the family of the church." But Josh and Paul had had ideas of thair own. They'd thought they'd sneak off and explore the woods and creek bottom instead. The pouring rain had complicated that.

"Hey, buddy, what's that on your forehead?" Josh said, staring at Paul.

"What do you mean?" Paul replied in mild annoyance. He rubbed his forehead. As he did, he looked casually at Josh. Suddenly he started laughing. "Man, look at your *own* forehead."

Suddenly they both found it important to be in front of a mirror. As they passed the other bunks, the other boys from Christ the Shepherd Church started pulling themselves out of bed. Before long there was a crowd at the mirror. Everybody in the room had a black smear across his forehead.

"Is that paint? Or ink? Or charcoal?" Josh asked, rubbing at the black mark on his forehead.

"Looks like felt pen. It's indelible, I think," said Paul disgustedly. "Do you suppose the girls got in here and did this while we were all asleep?"

"Dunno," said Josh, looking once more at his marked forehead in the glass. "But I'm going to find out. Come on. Let's go to breakfast."

It was a short, sloppy dash across the soaked yard to the dining hall. When they arrived, their hair already wet with rain, they caught the unmistakeable aroma of scrambled eggs and bacon. They were hungry enough to have forgotten completely about the strange markings on their foreheads. And perhaps they would have, had they not been stunned by what they saw when they sat down to eat.

Every girl from Christ the Shepherd Church had a black smear on her forehead too!

"I WANT EVERYBODY to break off in groups of four," said Pastor Dave. "You can pick your groups, but there have to be two boys and two girls in each one. If you don't want to do the choosing, I will."

Before the last two words were out of his mouth, there was a noisy scramble in the program room. Josh and Paul had already decided they would work together. But suddenly they had to find two girls to pair with them. Almost immediately they bumped into Cindy Thomas and Megan Anderson. Almost inseparable, the girls had had the same idea. They were looking for a couple boys to work with. With scarcely a word between the four of them, it was decided: they would be a team. Josh, Paul, Cindy and Megan grabbed four cushions from the pile in the corner and sat down on the floor, waiting for Pastor Dave's instructions.

"Okay, troops," Pastor Wassermann said, grinning, "It's time I came clean. Patty, the girls' counselor, and I are the guilty ones. We smeared the black marks on your foreheads last night while you were asleep."

A chorus of groans and mock complaints arose from around the room. Some of the girls wagged scolding fingers at Patty Fintel, the young adult counselor who had volunteered to come along for the weekend. Patty gave them an apologetic shrug, pointing to her own forehead, which also bore a black mark. Pastor Wassermann was wearing a black mark on his forehead as well.

"Here's the deal," the pastor said when the confusion began to fade out. "That black mark has something to do with the theme of this weekend. I'm not telling you — and neither is Patty — until one of you guesses correctly, what the mark is all about. Maybe you'll start to guess while we get into the discussion we're about to have."

A low rumble of conversation arose from the two dozen kids sitting on the floor cushions. Pastor Wassermann pressed forward: "Take your Bibles. Look up all the verses and stories you can think of — or find — that talk about Baptism. Then we want to have you talk, first in your groups of four, and then in our large group, about what you think any of those verses have to do with you and me today."

More chatter filled the room. Patty and the pastor started passing out Bibles from cardboard boxes in which they'd hauled them up to camp from the youth classroom back at Christ the Shepherd Church. Soon everybody was flipping pages, looking for stories about Baptism.

"I'll bet this black mark is s'posed to symbolize how

sinful everybody is," said Paul, turning the pages of his Bible. "And Baptism probably is what it takes to wash us clean. Do you think that's the deal?" he asked, looking at nobody in particular.

Megan Anderson said, "Where are we supposed to find stories about Baptism? I don't know that much about the Bible."

"How about that guy who baptized people in the Jordan River?" Josh suggested.

"Oh. Yeah. John," said Cindy, flipping to the book of Matthew. "That guy with the funny clothes. He lived out in the desert and ate grasshoppers."

"Locusts," said Megan.

Paul shrugged. "Yeah. Whatever. Anyhow, where is that in the Bible?"

"Matthew, chapter three," said Cindy, spotting the story and pointing to it.

The four read the story silently. When he was finished, Paul said, "I don't see much connection between this story and the world today. I mean, if Jesus was baptized once in a river somewhere, that's one thing. But what's that got to do with me?"

"That's true," said Cindy. "Jesus was God's Son. I'm not some special person like he was. His baptism was probably some special deal."

"You know something?" Josh said, leaning back and planting his hands on the floor behind him, "I don't even know when I was baptized. I mean, I know that I am. You have to be before they let you get confirmed. But I was just a baby. I don't remember the first thing about it. At least in this story, the people did it because they wanted it."

"I think you're right about the black mark though," said Megan. "Look. Here in the Bible story people came to get baptized because John told them they were dirty sinners. It was kind of like they all had black marks on their foreheads."

THERE WAS FREE TIME scheduled for two hours after lunch. Since the rain kept falling steadily, most of the kids from Christ the Shepherd Church had decided to go back to the program room and play records. Before he could get out of the dining room, however, Josh was intercepted by Pastor Dave Wassermann. "Can we talk for just a minute, Josh?" he said, gesturing toward a table near the corner of the room.

"Yeah. Sure. What's going on?" asked Josh, walking with the pastor toward the table.

"I . . . ah . . . I just had a phone call from your mother."

"My mom? She called you?"

The pastor nodded.

"Well . . . so what's the deal?"

Pastor Wassermann let out a heavy sigh. "This isn't going to be an easy thing to tell you, Josh."

Josh looked intently at him.

"Your mom . . . well, she asked me if I'd tell you that your dad left home last night, just after you took off to come up here. She says he isn't coming back."

Josh blinked. He wasn't sure he'd gotten it. "You mean . . . my folks are splitting up?"

"That's what your mother said. You didn't have a clue about it?"

Josh shook his head slowly. "No. They never mentioned anything. I never heard them fight or anything. How come? How come he left?"

"Your mother says he just got tired of being married. I'm sure there might be another side to the same story, if you'd ask your dad. But that's what your mom told me on the phone."

"How come she didn't phone me personally? How come she made you do it?" Josh was feeling confused and angry now.

"She said she was afraid to tell you. She didn't know if she could do it. And she said she didn't want to have you come home and discover what had happened, without any preparation for it or anything."

"Well, I think the whole thing stinks!" Josh said in a foul tone.

Pastor Wassermann nodded but did not reply. And Josh was glad he didn't.

IT WAS ALMOST suppertime when Pastor Dave found Josh. He had tromped through the wet forest for almost an hour, then had sat on a damp rock and sent stones he'd picked up sailing into the creek. He studied the results each time, watching the water splash up on the bank. The rain had kept falling the whole time, and by now he was almost soaked to his skin.

Pastor Wassermann sat down next to him and watched Josh throw stones for three or four minutes before he spoke. Then he said quietly, "You want to talk about it?"

Josh did not reply.

"It must be pretty rough getting a message like that. I can bet you're feeling pretty rotten just now. Am I right?"

"Darn right," growled Josh, throwing another stone.

"Josh, did you and your dad feel close to one another?"

Josh waited a long time before answering. Then he said, "You know, that's what really bugs me about all of this. My dad always acted as if I was somebody special. He used to tell me, no matter what, he'd always be there when I needed him." He gave a heavy sigh. "And now he takes off and just dumps my mom and me. And he does it when he knows I wouldn't be around or anything. He didn't even say goodbye. That really stinks."

They sat in silence once again. Then Pastor Wassermann said, "When people who say you can depend on them turn out not to be trustworthy, that's got to hurt a lot. That happened to me once when I was dating. This cute girl was going to marry me. At least, she said she was. I told all my friends. Then she found somebody who she thought would be earning lots more money than I would be as a pastor. So she dumped me."

Josh looked at Pastor Dave with surprise. He nodded, showing that he understood.

"You know, Josh, there's one person who will never let us down. You need to have at least one person like that in your life. When you and I were baptized, way back when we were too young to know about it or remember any of it, God made you and me a promise. He said he would stick by us no matter what. He put his mark on us when we were baptized. By the way, that's what these black marks are supposed to represent," he said, pointing to Josh's forehead, then his own. "So now you know the secret before any other kid in camp. The idea is, God's mark is there sort of like a stripe you can't get off. You see: you've been out here all afternoon, getting drenched in this rain. But still that black mark didn't come off. Oh, you'll get it off if you try hard enough. Try some strong soap. But God's mark never will come off. And that's the way God loves us. That's how faithful he is. Once we're baptized, he won't ever give up on us. Girlfriends may desert us. Even parents. God won't. That's why I'm glad I'm baptized. And that's why I hope you remember your baptism too."

Josh threw another stone into the river. He sat thinking. When he turned to look at Pastor Dave again, his eyes were wet. "Thanks," he said. "That helps. That helps a lot."

Pastor Dave Wasserman picked up one of Josh's stones and tossed it into the creek. "You hungry?" he asked quietly.

"Yeah," Josh said, getting up. "But I think I need to get out of these soaking clothes first."

"There's still time before we eat. Come on. I'll walk you back."

As they trudged along, Josh said, "How long do you think this black mark would stay on if I just left it and didn't try scrubbing it away?"

"Oh, I don't know. A week or so. Until you took a couple showers. I assume you do take showers, right?"

They both laughed. And the rain continued falling.

Thought and action starters:

1. Many Christians think your Baptism is useless unless you first decided that you wanted it. Josh found out otherwise. How could you respond to someone who said to you, "If you didn't ask to be baptized, it doesn't do you any good"?

2. Often people we thought we could count on don't prove to be faithful when we needed them. How many trustworthy people do you need in your life before you can "get through"? Which people are these in your own case just now?

3. Everybody celebrates their birthday. Have you ever thought of celebrating your baptismal day? Suppose the members of your family all began to do this.

A reading from Scripture that relates to this story is Matthew chapter three.

One Out of Ten

It may not make a lot of difference if you give in to group pressure and eat a chocolate-covered grasshopper — or even let somebody shave all the hair off your head. But what if everybody else is playing fast and loose with sex, and you're expected to join in?

Alex Carpenter had been good at sports since as long as he could remember. When his dad had put up the basketball hoop on the pole facing the driveway, way back when Alex was in fourth grade, he had taken to it with a vengeance. By the time he'd hit the seventh grade he was a deadly shot. It had helped that he was six foot even. When tryouts for junior varsity had been announced, Alex was sure he would be on the starting five. Not only did he make the squad, he had become the captain of the team.

Heading down to the locker room to change into his shorts and shoes for scrimmage, Alex heard familiar voices echoing behind him in the long school corridor. "Hey, Carpenter! Wait up!" Russ Hanson and Jerry Phillips soon were at his side, heading in the same direction.

"Our first game's with Southwest. Just found out," said Russ, who played guard opposite Alex on the starting five.

"They're tough this year," said Jerry, lanky center for the varsity. "At least, that's what I hear."

"That's what I hear too," said Alex, pushing through the door into the boys' locker room. "We'll handle 'em. Don't worry."

"Anything you say, boss," Russ answered in mock ridicule.

"We will," said Alex, sounding mildly annoyed.

"Let's go get 'em," said Buzz Gonzales, looking up from the bench where he sat, already suited up and tying his athletic shoes. Buzz and Larry Jones were the forwards on the starting five. Larry was already out on the court.

Alex's locker was directly across from the full-length mirror that was fastened to the wall beside the shower door. Alex had not had anything to do with getting the locker that he had this year. But, as he slid off his shoes and socks, and then stripped off his shirt and stepped out of his jeans, he found himself doing what he had done routinely before and after scrimmage these past few weeks: he studied himself in the mirror. As he stepped out of the last of his clothing he found himself admiring his smooth, athletic body. It was no wonder the girls at Lincoln High made eyes at him. He was a handsome kid. He knew it.

As he dressed for practice he wondered if Carrie Radnor had ever wondered what he might look like with no clothes on. He had dated Carrie for the past three months. In spite of everything, he'd had some less-than-pure thoughts about her from time to time. He'd even gotten more than friendly with her now and then on dates. And Carrie hadn't tried to stop him.

That had both excited and bothered Alex. His curiosity about sex was increasing by the day. And Carrie was a knockout. But he worried what might happen one of these nights if he tried to go too far with her and she encouraged him. He'd hate to get her pregnant or something.

Heading out onto the basketball court, Alex realized there was more to it than just the risk that he might get his girlfriend pregnant. He could still remember what Pastor Huesfloen had made them memorize in church class when Alex had been in catechism. For some reason, the words were still freshly etched into his memory:

We should fear and love God so that in matters of sex our words and actions are pure and honorable.

He wondered whether Martin Luther, who had written that, had ever had thoughts about making it with some girl when he had been the same age Alex was right now.

He'd never asked the pastor that. Somehow he didn't think that Pastor Huesfloen would know the answer.

Then the scrimmage started. Alex, Larry, Russ, Jerry and Buzz were teamed against a bunch of second-stringers. Even though the varsity was running them ragged, the other five put up a scrappy fight. Alex liked tough competition. It seemed to bring out the best in his game. As the sweat poured down his face and neck, and the sound of athletic shoes slapping the echoey floor and screeching from sudden starts and stops filled the room, he hit his stride. Today more than ever he was hitting long shots from the outside, seldom missing.

"Hey, way to hit 'em, Carpenter!" yelled Buzz Gonzales as the varsity increased its point spread.

"We're hot!" Alex shouted, grinning.

IN THE SHOWERS the five starters found themselves standing near one another. Russ Hanson said to Jerry Phillips, "Hey, lover, you made it with Janet Fenton yet?"

Jerry rubbed the soap across his chest and abdomen. He shook his head and frowned good-naturedly.

"You'd like to, wouldn't you?" Russ said, persisting.

Jerry shrugged.

"Well, listen up. Hey, you too, Carpenter . . . Gonzales . . . Jones," He said it with a careful voice that drew the five toward Russ Hanson's shower nozzle. "Look, guys, I just found out in the lunch room today that Becky's folks are taking off for the Thanksgiving weekend. Going to the Virgin Islands. Becky will be home alone three nights — Thursday, Friday, and Saturday."

"So?" Alex prodded.

"So this: she's having a party for about ten people. Guess which ten?"

"Us five, right?" Larry said, flicking a glob of soap off his arm.

"That's right. And Carrie, Janet, Sylvia and Tricia."

They were the girls the starting five on junior varsity had been dating this school year.

"So when's the party?" Jerry asked.

"On Friday night. And guess what, guys. The party ends

up with the lights off."

Buzz and Larry let out long, low whistles. Alex felt the hair stand on his neck.

"Her parents know?" asked Larry.

"Oh, sure," Russ replied sarcastically. "And she's taking out a full page advertisement in Sunday's paper." He paused for effect, then changed his tone to one of sternness and barked, "Of *course* they don't know, you jerk."

As he dried himself, Alex looked once more at his brown, athletic body in the full-length mirror. What would it be like to have Carrie Radnor see him like this? What would it be like for him to see her the same way, and to touch her anywhere he wanted?

Suddenly he wasn't sure he could go through with it. Or, if he could, he wasn't sure he should.

HE HAD TOLD HIS FOLKS he was going to a movie with Carrie. That gave Alex two or three hours he would not have to account for. Sitting next to her now, on one of the soft couches in the dimly-lit basement lounge in the Lane home, he felt his temperature rising. Carrie had unbuttoned his shirt and was trying to undo his belt. He had undone her blouse, much as he had done several other times on dates.

Becky Lane had already told each of the five couples which rooms and beds they could use if they wanted to. She and Russ Hanson had already gone off somewhere. Jerry and Janet Fenton were on another couch. Buzz and Sylvia McDonald were stretched out nearby on the carpet. Larry and Tricia Miller were getting themselves soft drinks from the refrigerator at the other end of the long basement room.

Alex wanted to take Carrie's blouse off. But something kept him from doing it. Perhaps it was the thought of getting Carrie pregnant, Or perhaps it was those words from Martin Luther. Or perhaps it was that report he had heard this evening on the radio, while he'd been stretched out on his bed at home. The newscaster had said that lots of people were now getting AIDS; in fact, it was becoming a nationwide epidemic; it could kill you; there was no known cure; and intimate sexual contact was one way it was spreading.

"Carrie?"

"Mmmm?" She had succeeded in unbuckling his jeans.

"Carrie, what if you or I get AIDS or something doing this?" He said it softly so that only she could hear.

"Not likely," she replied, smoothing her fingers across his smooth chest. "I'm still a virgin. Aren't you?"

"Well . . . yeah . . . but . . ."

"But what?"

"Well . . . I think we're taking a big risk."

She sat up, backed off, sighed heavily, and said, "Oh, cripes, Alex. You're not going to do it, are you!"

Alex gave her a confused look. "No. I guess I'm not."

"Well that's just great," she muttered. "Because there are eight other people here who probably are."

"Yeah. I'm sorry."

"Sure," she said sarcastically. "Well, what would you think if I just waited for Buzz to get through with Sylvia. Or Larry, when he's done with Tricia?" There was anger and impatience in her voice.

"Listen, I don't . . . I don't know." He felt as though he had betrayed her. But he knew if he went through with it he would betray himself. "Look, Carrie, I can't tell you what you ought to do. I just know I can't do this. I'm . . . honestly, I'm sorry."

He didn't hear what she said next, if she said anything. Somehow he found his way out of the darkened basement and upstairs, down the front hall, and outside to the porch, all without turning on a light. The whole way home he wondered what he would say when he saw Carrie the next time.

When he got home he discovered his folks had gone out. He was relieved. He went into the basement, got onto the exercise machine he and his dad both used sometimes, and pumped at the rowing handles until he thought he would pass out from sheer exhaustion. Then he went upstairs and took a long, cool shower.

THAT SUNDAY in church, Pastor Huesfloen read a story from the Gospel of Saint Luke. Ten men, dying of an incurable disease, had all been suddenly healed and had gone home to show themselves to their astounded relatives. But only one came back to thank Jesus for healing them. "Where are the nine?" Jesus asked when the tenth one came to show his gratitude.

Alex thought about the ten people who had been there in Becky Lane's basement. What had happened to the other nine? What were they saying about him? What would they say to him at scrimmage Monday afternoon?

He vaguely heard the pastor's sermon. It was something about giving thanks for things we take for granted. Alex spent the sermon time praying a long, intense prayer of thanksgiving. "Thanks, Lord," he said silently, "for giving me a conscience. And for stuff I've learned here in this church, that keeps me from doing things I'd regret. And thanks for sticking by me when I stray into temptation. And, Lord, thanks for giving me a second chance whenever I do — or think — something that's not worthy of somebody that you love and care about and died for."

When he whispered his "Amen" he felt as though he knew how those ten fellows had felt, getting rid of leprosy. He was convinced it was at least as good as it would feel to score the winning basket against Southwest the week after next.

Thought and action starters:

1. Sex can be a powerful force inside us. Do you think God overdid it when he gave us so much sexual energy and curiosity? What do you think he may have had in mind by making it so strong?

2. Is there a difference between imagining what you could do with your sexuality and actually doing it? Suppose your thoughts keep turning to doing things you are sure are wrong: what do you think God would want you to do about it?

3. Alex took a real risk walking out on nine people who expected him to do the same things they were doing. Have you ever done something courageous like that? How did things work out?

A reading from Scripture that relates to this story is Romans 12:1-2. A second is Luke 17:11-19.

A Sudden Sacrifice

If someone does something to make you mad enough, is it okay to get revenge? Suppose it could get them into ten times as much trouble as they caused you?

Jon Simpson shifted in his desk chair. He was having trouble keeping even one ear tuned to what Miss Jackson was explaining at the chalkboard. His head was still pounding.

Across the aisle, in the next row, Eddie Schwartz was leaning over a sheet of notebook paper on his desk. How, Jon wondered, could Eddie be so interested in algebra all of a sudden? Eddie had never done well in this class.

At this moment Jon's feelings toward Eddie were not fit to be repeated out loud. If it hadn't been for Eddie, Jon would not have ended up with a scolding from the principal half an hour ago. It was Eddie's fault. Jon was convinced of it.

Eddie was always pulling some smart-aleck stunt. When he got you into trouble he would brag about it. But if he was cornered by a teacher or the principal, he'd lie and say he hadn't done it.

Up to now Jon hadn't gotten caught in Eddie's trap. But last hour it had finally happened. In gym class, while they had been out shooting baskets, somebody had gone back into the locker room and taken Jon's socks. After his shower, Jon had been unable to get dressed. He'd wasted fifteen minutes looking for his missing socks. That had made him late to algebra, and landed him in the principal's office.

"Now let's take a closer look at this equation," Miss

Jackson said, turning to the chalkboard. Jon could not have been less interested in equations. The thing that made him maddest about Eddie was that, as Eddie had gone out of the locker room, he'd said, "You might have dropped 'em in the toilet by mistake." Sure enough, after looking everywhere else, that's where Jon had found his socks. Even though the water in the stool looked clean, and even though he'd been able to wring his socks almost dry before putting them back on, the whole thing made him madder than blue blazes — at Eddie.

"Eddie, let's have you try the next problem," said Miss Jackson suddenly.

Eddie looked up with a hint of panic on his face. He slid the piece of notebook paper under his math book and got out of his seat.

Jon watched Eddie head up to the chalkboard. Then he glanced across the aisle to Eddie's desk. The note paper was sticking out. Jon looked around him. Nobody was watching. Quietly and quickly he pulled the paper across to his own desk. Rapidly he scanned the words. Whatever this was, it was definitely not algebra!

In fact, it was a letter. "Dear Miss Jackson," it began. It sounded to Jon like a love letter. But then he realized exactly what it was. Eddie had written a whole page of embarrassing — in fact, obscene and filthy — things he was imagining he'd like to do with the algebra teacher. Reading it, Jon's face turned hot. Eddie had even signed his full name at the bottom.

Eddie was still at the chalkboard when the bell rang. Folding up the paper, Jon hid it inside his pants pocket. Gathering his books, he headed out the door. On the way home, Eddie caught up to him.

"You ... didn't happen to see a piece of notebook paper on my desk in algebra," he said, sounding uncomfortable.

"What sort of paper?" Jon asked innocently, hiking steadily along.

"Just ... just a ... nothing, really ... just ..."

"I don't think I saw anything like that," said Jon, still feeling an annoying dampness in his socks.

AT SUPPER, Jon's father said, "Pastor Wilson called. He needs you to light the candles at church tonight."

"Tonight! Dad, this is Wednesday! It's the middle of the week!"

"It's also the first day of Lent, Jon. We have a church service at 7:30. I told Pastor Wilson you could do it."

AT TWENTY MINUTES after seven, as he slipped into his robe, Jon realized he still had Eddie's letter in his pocket. All through Pastor Wilson's sermon he wondered what he should do with it. He figured he would seal it in an envelope and slip it into Miss Jackson's mailbox at school. That would cook Eddie's goose for good.

"You may have wondered," Pastor Wilson said, looking out at the congregation, "why I have this charcoal burner standing up here by the pulpit. No, we aren't going to cook hamburgers after church." The congregation laughed politely. "But we are planning to have a fire tonight. In fact, I checked with the city fire marshal and he said it was okay."

Jon sat up and began to pay attention.

"You'll remember," said the pastor, "that in the book of Romans, Saint Paul says we should forgive our enemies, even while we repent of our own sins. By doing that we're heaping burning coals on their heads. You see, if you've done something cruel to me, and I repay you with love and forgiveness, that's a painful thing for you to handle. You can't keep on hating me for very long."

Jon thought of Eddie. Forgive him? Forget it!

"This is what I want you all to do," said Pastor Wilson. "Take one of those slips of paper you find in the hymnal rack in front of you. On it write some sin you're sorry for and want to get rid of. Or, write down something somebody has done to hurt you, something that you're ready to forgive."

Everybody started taking slips of paper from the hymnal racks and pulling out their pens or pencils.

"After all of you are finished," Pastor Wilson said, "I want you all to bring your slips of paper up and drop them in the burner here. Then I'm going to ask Jon Simpson to set all of them on fire. Tonight is Ash Wednesday. This is how we'll make our ashes."

Jon was caught off guard. The pastor hadn't told him he would have this extra task tonight.

The organ started playing. People started coming forward. Soon the charcoal burner was piled high with slips of paper. Jon stepped to the altar. With his candle lighter he took fire from one of the candles, carried it to the burner, and set the slips on fire. As he did it he heard Pastor Wilson start to pray, "Lord, let our prayers rise up to you, just as this fire is rising."

Jon watched the paper turn to ashes, crumbling inside the protective aluminum foil Pastor Wilson had put around the edges.

Then, as the flame began to drop, he slipped Eddie Schwartz' letter out of his pocket and added it to the fire.

Tomorrow, he decided, he would set Eddie's mind at ease about it. And maybe he would even tell him he forgave him for swiping his socks in gym class.

Thought and action starters:

1. "Don't get angry, just get even" is a slogan many people use. What do you think of it? How have you felt the times you've tried to follow it?

2. Psychologists say that revenge is the most destructive of all human emotions. Why do you suppose that is? Jesus' death on the cross was God's way of showing us that love is better than revenge. How have you found that to be true with people you have difficulty tolerating?

3. Next time you're at worship and the congregation is participating in a service for confession of sins, try to make your own list of things to confess as specific as possible. You may want to start the list, at least in your own mind, before you get to church.

A reading from Scripture that relates to this story is Psalm 51:1-13. Another is Romans 12:14-21.

A Miracle at One O'clock

Parents can be hard to figure out sometimes. But parents have real troubles of their own. Kim Jacobs found that to be true with her own mother.

Kim was getting angry. Her mother should have been here almost half an hour ago. The other members of her Sunday class had all gone home. Almost all the teachers had gone by this time. For all she knew, she was the only person left inside the building at First Plymouth Church.

She paced up and down, staring impatiently out the big plate glass window, surveying the parking lot. Her mother never was so late. Why couldn't she have phoned or something?

She heard the clack-clack-clack of high heels coming down the hallway. Straightening her posture, she smoothed back her blond hair, trying to look as though she had some good reason to be standing here in the empty entryway.

"Kim! I think you're the last one," said Mrs. Jones. Kim gave a weak smile and nodded at her Sunday class teacher.

"Waitin' for my mom. She's just a little late, I guess."

"I could give you a ride. You want me to? It's not too many blocks out of my way."

"Uh . . . no . . . no, if you did she might come and not know what happened to me. I'll just wait. Thanks anyway."

"Well, okay then, I think you're the last person in the building, though. Just double-check, when you go out, to see the door is latched behind you. It will lock behind you as you leave."

"Okay. Thanks. See you."

"Have a good day, Kim," said Mrs. Jones, clack-clacking across the linoleum toward the double glass front doors. Kim heard them close and lock behind her as she left the building.

Now she really *was* alone. Just her, deserted, locked inside First Pilgrim Church. Where *was* her mother, anyway?

She watched the blue Buick roll out of the church lot. Mrs. Jones would probably be half done eating dinner before Kim's mother even got to the church. Kim wondered if her Sunday teacher had a clue about Kim's mother. Probably not. Kim hadn't said a word about it. And she knew her mother wasn't one to pass around personal things, like her bad health. Sometimes Kim wished her mother would have been more open about things.

It probably would take a miracle to change the way her mother was, she realized. The words of Mrs. Jones crept back into Kim's head. She'd heard them just an hour ago in class: "Sometimes God does a miracle and we don't even know it."

Kim kicked at the brick wall, hurting her big toe. She wondered, if she had her choice, which miracle she'd rather have: for God to cure the cancer that her mom just found out Thursday she was probably going to die from; or for her mom to show some warmth and love to her, just once before she died.

Kim knew the answer. She would rather have the love.

She looked once more out to the parking lot. It was almost 12:50 now. No sign of a brown station wagon. "Darn!" she said, turning and trudging back to the soft couch by the magazine rack. Slouching down on it, she picked up a book of devotion's. Flopping through the pages, she stopped turning at a page entitled "Too Many Miracles." She noticed the paragraph just above the prayer: "Miracles won't make us trust and love God. Listening to God speak in our hearts, and saying yes to God's truth when we hear it, will."

She looked up at the big green banner on the wall across the room. "God cares for you," it said. She thought about it for a second. "Well, God, if you care so much, what are you going to do about my mom?" Her question echoed off the walls. She said it louder, then shouted it: "What, God? What!" It sounded strange to hear her voice bounce back at her. It felt strange, shouting in a church building.

She looked back at the printed page. She read the prayer: "Lord, make us stop wanting to see more miracles. Help us believe in you, feel your love for us, and love you in return."

"What is this 'more miracles' garbage?" she muttered, tossing the magazine back on the table. "I haven't ever seen the first one."

She looked at the clock on the wall, above the drinking fountain. Seven before one. Where was her mother?

Then she saw the car, coming across the parking lot. Kim jumped up, hurried to the front door, let herself out, and checked to be sure the door would latch behind her.

When she got into the car, before she had a chance to scold her mother, she could see she had been crying. Then her mom turned off the key, covered her eyes with her hands, and started shaking. There was no sound. Just shaking.

Kim was frightened. She had never seen her mother cry. A lot of times she'd wished her mother would have, but she never had in front of Kim.

Her mother finally turned to her and said, "Kim . . . I got really sick this morning. For a little while I didn't know if I was going to make it."

Kim felt chills run down her spine.

"The doctor warned me I could have some bad times, now that it's getting worse."

The "it" was cancer. Her mother never called it cancer, only "it."

"Kim, that's why I was late. I . . . didn't feel strong enough for a while to get out to the car. I'm . . . doing better now."

"Oh, that's okay, Mom. It was no big deal," Kim said, wishing what she was saying now was not a lie.

"Listen, Kim," her mother answered, giving her a serious look, "I got to thinking . . . just this morning, I . . . I could die at any time. I know that. So do you. You know, I'd hate to die and never have told you how much I . . .

just how much I love you."

Tears were streaming down Kim's mother's face. Kim moved closer and gave her mother a firm hug. She felt herself shaking the way her mother had been just a few minutes before.

On the way home Kim heard the words run through her head again, the words that Mrs. Jones had given her in Sunday class: "Sometimes God does a miracle and we don't even know it."

"Thanks, God," she said quietly.

"What was that, Kim? You say something?" asked her mother.

"Uh . . . yeah. I said, 'Thanks,' Mom. Thanks . . . for the miracle."

Thought and action starters:

1. Every kid who's ever lived has wondered why he or she couldn't understand his or her parents. There's good evidence most parents feel the same way about their own children. Sometime when you have an opportunity, surprise one or both of your parents by inviting them to respond to this: "Mom, Dad, what things worry you the most?" Or: "Mom, Dad, I'll bet you are really hurting sometimes. Could you tell me about any of those times?" (Don't be surprised if they faint the first time you try that, but stick with it until you get a good conversation going.)

2. Have you ever wondered what your parents' lives were like when they were the exact same age as you are now? The world was different then, of course. But you might be amazed to learn how much things haven't changed. Some time when you have time to talk, ask them to tell you about what they can remember about their life then.

3. Have you ever talked with other people in your family about how you could cope with the situation if somebody in your family circle came down with a life-threatening disease? How could you help them cope if you were the one?

A reading from Scripture that relates to this story is Mark 3:1-5.

Easter Jones

Everybody knows that alcohol and gasoline don't mix. But what would you do if you saw a pair of headlights, wildly swerving on the highway in the middle of the night, and coming your direction?

Jennie Simonson looked across the cafe booth at Carrie Jones. She waited for her to finish her Coke Classic before she said, "Okay, let's have it. Something's on your mind or you wouldn't have bought this Coke for me."

Carrie tossed her curly blond hair and flashed a mysterious expression at her freckle-faced companion. "Shadow's pregnant," she said with a sudden smirk.

Jennie blinked, then answered, "What? She's what?"

"She's pregnant!"

Jennie said, "You mean that's all this is about? To tell me that your dog is pregnant?"

Carrie swirled the Coke in the bottom of the chilled can. Looking at the ring of water the can had created on the table top, she said, "Well . . . no. Of course it isn't. But Shadow *is* pregnant. I just want you to know that."

"Okay. I believe you. So what else?"

"Well . . . look. I don't know how to say this to you."

"I'm your best friend, right?"

"Right."

"Then just *say* it."

Carrie took a deep breath. "Okay. Here goes," she said, shifting in her seat. "Jen, I'm worried about you."

"No kidding. Why?" She said it dryly, as though guessing what was coming.

"Come on, Jen. You know."

"It's Dean Walsh, right?"

"Of course. Jennie, you're not even out of junior high school yet. You run around with somebody like him and you'll end up an alcoholic."

"Like my brother Mark, right?"

"Well, I guess maybe."

"Look, Carrie, just because you don't touch alcohol doesn't mean you have to give me a hard time about it. I can handle it, okay?"

Carrie looked at her empty Coke can, turning it slowly on the table top. "I guess I knew you'd take offense if I said anything. I'm only saying it because I like you. That's all."

"Well, I wish you'd just lay off," said Jennie sullenly. "Why can't you just live and let live?"

Carrie turned her own can around and around in the puddle of water. "You know she said, "that's kind of weird."

"What is?"

"To hear you say 'live and let live.' Just yesterday in church Pastor Jordain — you do remember Pastor Jordain, right? — "

"Knock it off," said Jennie, half annoyed, half grinning. "I still go to church . . . once in a while."

"Well, anyway, Pastor Jordain said if Jesus had said 'Live and let live,' he wouldn't have died on the cross for us. And next Sunday wouldn't be Easter. We might never have found out about eternal life or anything."

"Look," Jennie said impatiently, "my family's going to be at Easter service next Sunday. Even Mark, my juvenile delinquent brother."

Carrie stopped turning the can. Getting up, she said, "Okay, okay. Look, Jen, I gotta go. I just thought you'd like to know about Shadow."

"Yeah. Thanks for telling me," said Jennie, getting up with her.

"See you tomorrow," Carrie said, heading for the cash register.

WEDNESDAY NIGHT at nine o'clock, while she was climbing into bed, Jennie heard the phone ring. Somebody answered it. There were muffled voices in the dining room. After what seemed like a long time, her parents both appeared at the door of her bedroom. Jennie sat up in bed and waited for something to happen. Neither of her parents said anything. They just stood looking at her.

"Well . . . ?" Jennie said. "What's going on?" Then she realized her mother's eyes were wet. "Mom? Dad? . . . " She said, straightening against the headboard.

Her father didn't move. Her mother came closer and sat down in the chair next to the bed. She had a look of terror on her face. She said, "Jennie . . . " Then she took a deep breath. "Oh, my God," she said, how am I going to tell you this?" She broke down and began to sob uncontrollably.

Jennie looked at her father. He pressed his lips together and closed his eyes. She'd never seen him do that before.

Her mother found a kleenex, blew her nose, found another one, and tried to dry her eyes. Then she said, "Jennie, this is a horrible thing to tell you in the middle of the night. But you have to know."

"Is it about Mark?" she asked, flashing a frightened look.

"No. It isn't Mark."

"Well . . . ?"

"It's . . . Carrie."

Jennie's eyes grew larger. "What about her."

"Something's happened. Something terrible."

There was no mistaking what her mother meant to say. "Oh, God!" cried Jennie. Her mother nodded miserably. Jennie shrieked until she thought her lungs would burst.

SHE DIDN'T GO to school the rest of the week. Her mother stayed home from work to be with her. Jennie felt numb. It seemed to her she heard her mother say it fifty times as least: "I just can't understand why God would let a drunk teenager run down Carrie Jones. Of all the families in this town, the Joneses have to be the most religious."

It seemed strange to have a funeral on the day before Easter. Pastor Jordain talked about new life and how Carrie's life was just beginning. Jennie was sure that her own was over.

On Easter morning Pastor Jordain mentioned Carrie in his sermon. The church seemed unusually crowded. Was it because of Carrie? Or was it because it was Easter? Jennie decided maybe some of both. One thing she remembered hearing in the sermon was: "Until we let die something we love very much, we cannot have new life."

It didn't make much sense to her.

On the way out of church, Carrie's mother spotted Jennie. It was hard for her to get through the crowds of people, but she finally made it. Jennie didn't know what in the world she ought to say to her. Mrs. Jones took care of that. When she caught up with Jennie, she just gave her a warm smile. Not saying anything, she gave Jennie a hug and held on for what seemed like half a minute. Afterwards Jennie could see her eyes were glistening.

The next week school dragged for Jennie. In her classes she sat thinking about the teenager from out of town who'd had too much to drink. She wondered if he'd seen Carrie when he ran the red light. Sometimes she even imagined that Dean Walsh had been the driver.

The next Sunday she and both her parents went to church. The Sunday after that her mother went with her. The third Sunday nobody wanted to get up. She went alone. In fact, she found her mother's confirmation Bible, tucked away inside the piano bench, and took it with her. After church she stayed and went to class — the one that Carrie would have gone to. The girl sitting next to her whispered, "Nice to see you. I thought you had given up on Sunday class."

"You guys prob'ly thought I died or something, right?" she whispered back.

"Well, it's still the Easter season. It's a good time to start something new I guess."

ON SATURDAY the phone rang. Jennie answered.

"This is Carrie's mother. I just thought you'd like to know that Shadow had her pups this week. I asked your mother and she said she'd let me give you one. That is, if you would like one."

"Would I ever! Thank you, Mrs. Jones. Thanks very much." She had forgotten about Shadow all these weeks. Still, before she'd hung up, she knew just exactly what she'd call her brand new cocker spaniel:

Easter. Easter Jones.

Thought and action starters:

1. Alcohol consumption is a big problem in the public schools. So is teenage drunken driving. Have you had a "close call" due to alcohol and driving (regardless who was behind the wheel)? How could you (did you) console those who have lost a loved one in this way?

2. The national organization, "Mothers Against Drunk Driving" (M.A.D.D.), has given rise to "Students Against Drunk Driving" (S.A.D.D.). Is there such a group in your school? Should there be? How could you help to get one established?

3. There is a verse in a familiar hymn that asks God to help us to "fear the grave as little as our bed." What do you know and believe as a Christian that makes this a possibility for you?

A reading from Scripture that relates to this story is 1 Corinthians chapter fifteen.

The Winner and Still Champion

Can you technically obey the rules but still end up winning dishonestly? An athlete who was cutting corners in the classroom had to ask himself that question.

Skip Templeton chugged along, driving himself uphill. He felt an electric surge of excitement run through him as he neared the crest of Hill Street. This was the exact route of the All-City-Schools competition, just a week away. He knew he would be one of the best runners in the competition. Lots of people were saying he would win hands down. Getting up Hill Street would probably sort out the winner from the losers.

Chung, chung, chung. His Nikes hit the pavement in relentless rhythm. *Chung, chung, chung.* He was near the top now. *Chung, chung.* Skip felt perspiration soaking his scalp, underneath his crop of handsome curly chestnut hair. More perspiration rivered down his back. His underarms were soaked. But he felt wonderful. Exhilarated, even. His body felt so well-tuned he hardly could believe it. Running every day after school for a month could do that to a guy.

Reaching the crest of Hill Street, he surged forward to the lamp post where he knew the race would end next week. Raising his arms above his head as he ran past the marker, he thought to himself, "The winner and still champion!"

AT HOME, SKIP FOUND a note his mother had left on the kitchen table. "All of us have eaten. Supper's in the oven. Tess called." He exhaled with exhaustion. He'd lost track of time again. The clock showed twenty after seven. No wonder he'd missed supper. But it took time to get ready for a competition like All-City-Schools.

He checked the oven. Meatloaf. He went into the hall and dialed a familiar number. While he waited for an answer he lifted his sweaty shirt away from his damp body.

"Hello, Tess?"

"Skip? I've been waiting for an hour for you to call me back."

"Been running."

"All this time?"

"Got to. Can't take a chance on losing next week."

"Have you studied for the history test?"

"When is that? Monday?"

"No. Tomorrow, dummy."

"Oh, wow! Yikes. You kidding me?"

"No kidding. You're not ready, are you?"

"Well . . . not quite."

"Have you read any of it?"

"Come on, Tess."

"Well, have you?"

"Well . . . no. Actually, I haven't."

"I suggest you come over and study with me for a while."

"Tonight?"

"No, Saturday, stupid."

When Tess called him "dummy" or "stupid" in her soft and teasing voice, it sounded like poetry to Skip. He saw her in his imagination, her soft black hair setting off her brown eyes and her cute, round face. No wonder she was head cheerleader. And the president of junior youth at church.

"Look, I still gotta shower. And then eat. How 'bout if I come over around eight?"

"You'd have to leave by nine. I thought maybe you could come sooner."

"Well, maybe a quarter of eight, then. Just let me get my shower or you won't see me at all."

"Okay. See you when you get here."

Skip took his time beneath the spray. Nothing felt quite as good to him as a relaxing shower after long, hard exercise. As he was drying off, he looked at his handsome face in the vanity mirror. He was really good looking, he decided. No wonder Tess liked him. That and the fact that he was such a star runner.

For some reason his thoughts turned to Andy Thomas. Andy was the only other runner in the school — maybe in the city — who could compete with Skip. But Andy was a loser's loser in most other ways. Bad breath. Tall and skinny. Dandruff. Acne. Not a single girl was interested in Andy. Little wonder. But he was a speedy runner. Maybe it was those long, long legs of his.

"YOU KNOW WHAT I THINK?" said Tess. brushing the hair back from her eyes.

"No, what?" asked Skip, absently flipping the pages in his history book.

"I think you're in bad shape for that exam tomorrow. Skip, you haven't studied *any* of this!"

"Yeah . Well . . . just keep talking. I'm beginning to catch on."

"Skip, you'll be lucky to get a D minus."

"Honest, I thought this test wasn't until Monday."

"Well, you thought wrong. And if you don't pass it . . . "

"Yeah. I know. I can't run in the competition."

"You know something, Skip? I'll bet you haven't studied for any of your classes for over a month."

Skip shrugged good-naturedly. "Too busy. And besides, I can get by most of the time."

"But you had A's until the running season started. Now you're getting C's. What do your folks say about that?"

"They're not thrilled exactly. But Dad's counting on me to win next week. And after that I'll hit the books again. I still can get my averages up to A minus if I really push it."

"Well, you'll have a hard time wiping out an F in history."

"Come,on, Tess. Give me a break. Just tell me exactly what I have to know. That's what I'll study. I'm too tired to read all the assignments."

"You'd be up all night if you *did* try. There are seven chapters." She gave Skip of a disapproving look. He saw a hint of doom in her eyes. It gave him a feeling of mild panic.

"Oh, all right," she said in resignation. "Here is what you probably will have to know. Just write this down . . . "

IN SUNDAY CLASS Skip took the chair Tess had saved for him, next to her. "I told you everything would be okay," he said.

It was too smug-sounding for her. "The only reason Mrs. Carnes gave you a C was because I told you exactly what to study." The hoarse whisper had a scolding tone, but she dissolved it with a grin.

"Class," said Rick, the discussion leader, "Tell me what you think of this from the New Testament." Rick studied the page in his Bible for a moment, then began to read:

No soldier on service gets entangled in civilian pursuits, since his aim is to satisfy the one who enlisted him. An athlete is not crowned unless he competes according to the rules. It is the hard-working farmer who ought to have the first share of the crops.

"Now which of those ideas applies best to this class?" Rick asked, looking around the room. A snicker arose from somewhere. "Dumb question," said a boy across the table from Skip.

"How about an intelligent answer then?" asked Rick good-naturedly.

"That part about the athlete, obviously," the boy replied in a bored tone.

"His parents make him come," said Tess, whispering carefully. "I'm sure he'd rather be home in bed."

It occurred to Skip he himself had never come to class before Tess had started coming.

"Okay," said Rick, looking at Skip. "We've got at least one athlete here. Skip, tell us what you think that sentence from Second Timothy is really saying."

"Ah . . . would you read it again, please?" Skip said,

caught by surprise.

"You have a Bible, Skip?"

"Ah . . . yeah. I'm looking on with Tess here." More snickers could be heard from the others, all of whom had brought their Bibles with them.

"Okay. Listen," Rick said, looking at his Bible once again. "An athlete is not crowned unless he competes according to the rules'."

Skip turned it over in his mind. Suddenly, in his imagination, he was chugging up Hill Street again. This time he could hear the crowds from his school cheering him on. "Ah . . . well, just what it says, I guess," he said, looking at Rick.

"Try putting it in your own words."

Skip shifted in his chair. He looked at the words above where Tess had her finger placed on the page. "Well . . . like with the All-City-Schools competition next week. There's only one approved course to run. You have to run exactly that course or else you'll be disqualified."

"Okay. Right on," said Rick. "Now let's apply that to our Christan faith."

Skip wasn't thinking about Christian faith. He was thinking about the long, exhausting course he had to run this coming week. His heart began to pound just thinking about it. In his imagination he saw skinny Andy Thomas gaining on him as they reached the base of the incline on Hill Street. He imagined Andy started to drop back as they went up, because Andy had not built up as much endurance as Skip had. That was exactly where he would beat him. He was sure of it.

As class was breaking up, Skip said to Tess, "Oh, by the way, did anybody hear how Andy Thomas did in history Friday?"

"Like he always does," said Tess. "He got an A."

IT WAS EXACTLY as Skip had imagined it would be. The All-City-Schools competition had turned out to be a two-man race. Just he and Andy were competing as they reached the steepest part of Hill Street. And, just as he had known he would, Skip felt a surge of reserve energy as he began to pull away from Andy, going up. *Chung, chung, chung* went his Nikes on the pavement. In his mind's eye he saw cheering students just beyond the hillcrest. He imagined Tess was in the front row, cheering loudest of them all. He wondered if Rick, the youth leader would be watching. Then something from Sunday class ran through his mind again. "An athlete is not crowned unless he competes according to the rules." Why did that bother him? He'd followed all the rules. *Hadn't he?*

Maybe it was the sound of Andy's shoes and his heavy breathing somewhere back behind Skip that made everything click in his mind. Andy had not trained for this as much as Skip had. But Andy had followed the rules. He'd passed the history test with flying colors. On the other hand, Tess had given Skip help. He knew he would have flunked it if she hadn't. In one way, Skip knew he had cheated Andy. And probably himself.

Perhaps that was what made him start to slow his pace. Andy started getting closer. Then they both were neck and neck. Then Skip slowed to a walk and waved Andy on past. Skip heard the crowd roar for Andy even before he himself was at the summit. Just before he reached the hillcrest, Skip began to run again. He didn't hear his classmates' jeers and catcalls as he came in a poor second.

What he *did* hear was his conscience. It was saying, "Okay Skip, so you lost the race. But in the process you have gotten back your self respect."

And by golly, in the future I intend to hang onto it, Skip muttered to himself, as his pace slowed to a walk. When he saw Tess, he was relieved to see her smiling.

Thought and action starters:

1. You may have heard your school teachers say "If you cheat by taking answers from other students, you are stealing from them and cheating yourself." In what way is that true?

2. In spite of his lousy study habits, Skip Templeton really had developed a good discipline for physical fitness. How are you doing in that department? Does it require an expensive gym set in your basement? Think about some ways you could begin to get yourself into better condition in the next six months.

3. One person (an adult) who read this story said, "I don't believe a teenage athlete — even one with a sensitive conscience — would slow down and deliberately lose a race the way Skip Templeton did." What do you think?

A reading from Scripture that relates to this story is 1 Corinthians 9:23-27. Another is 2 Timothy 2:1-7.

Something Old, Something New

Jan Fletcher knew the church she went to wasn't the world's most exciting. But she wasn't sure she was quite ready to exchange it for her best friend's denomination, with its offer of emotional experience.

As soon as she heard the garage door slam shut and the crunch of the tires on the gravel driveway outside her bedroom window, Jan Fletcher thought she could feel the fever starting to go away. Sitting up in bed, she watched as the car carrying her parents and her younger brother and sister disappeared, around the corner of the neighbor's garage, on their way to church.

It was the first time Jan had ever missed church since she'd started confirmation instruction at Trinity Church. A couple times, back in the fourth grade, she'd stayed home because of sickness. But, since starting the junior high class for kids planning to be confirmed, she'd never missed. They gave you the impression that if you didn't come on Sundays while that class was running, you'd be kicked out of the church. Jan knew that wasn't really true, but her folks had made sure she'd always been there.

But the class was over now. She had been confirmed for three months. They didn't really hassle you to go as much after you were confirmed. Her folks kept going, of course, and never had even hinted that maybe Jan could drop out or anything. Until today.

Climbing from bed, she pulled a robe on, went into the living room, and turned on the TV. She felt a little guilty, staying home and watching television while her family was at church. But, honestly, she really *had* thought she had a fever. Even her mom had thought so. Jan flipped the dial. Nothing seemed to be on except religion programs. Big choirs singing in huge auditoriums. Preachers wearing fancy suits.

Then suddenly she stopped. On channel nine she caught sight of a preacher who looked vaguely familiar to her. Of course! It was the preacher at the City Temple, where one of her two best friends went. She'd seen his picture on a worship folder Liz Carstenson had given her at school a couple months ago.

Liz had tried to get Jan to come with her to City Temple several times. She'd never gone with her. The way Liz talked, the pastor at her church — or "temple," as she always called it — was incredible. Well, Jan thought, settling back into the soft couch, tucking her feet up underneath her robe, this might be her chance to find out.

The pastor was almost finished with his message, from the sound of it. He kept repeating something from the Bible text he'd chosen for the sermon: "You must be born again." She'd heard the pastor in her own church say that now and then. And Jan had really thought, once she had been confirmed, that she would get a different feeling about God and church and things. But it had been three months since she had stood up at the altar, promising to be faithful. Things hadn't seemed to change much since then.

That bothered Jan a little.

TUESDAY AFTERNOON, at J.C. Penney's, looking for a blouse, she bumped into Liz and their mutual girlfriend, Kerri Wagner. "Let's go get a Pepsi or something," said Kerri, after all three were finished browsing in Penney's. In the booth they chattered for a while about the boys they hadn't seen since school had let out for the summer. Then Kerri, sucking the last of her drink out of the glass with a noisy crackle, jumped up, saying, "Gotta run. Take care, you two."

When she was gone, Liz said to Jan, "That kid has energy to burn."

"No kidding," Jan said, grinning.

"I just wish she'd use a little of it on somebody besides herself."

"What do you mean?"

"Do you realize she spent seventeen dollars in Penney's today?"

"So?"

"So, every time I'm anywhere with her it's always like that. Once I asked her if she ever gave any of her allowance to a church or anything."

"Nice try. You know she doesn't belong anywhere."

"Yeah," said Liz, frowning. Suddenly she brightened. "Hey, our minister had one teriffic sermon Sunday."

"I know. I heard some of it."

Liz looked wide-eyed at her. "You . . . you what?"

"Don't get your hopes up," Jan said, grinning. "I heard it on television."

"Oh, hey, neat. But . . . you would have had to miss your own church to do that."

"Yeah. I had a fever Sunday."

"Look, we're having a prayer service at the Temple tomorrow night. Do you think your folks would let you come?"

Liz had never put it that way before. " 'Let me'? I don't have to ask permission." There was mild annoyance in her voice.

"Oh, I figured you never came with me because your folks were set against it.

"Look, I've got a church, okay?"

"I know. But I've been to your church. If you'll pardon my saying so, it's sort of boring. It almost put me to sleep."

"It's . . . just more traditional, that's all." As soon as she said it, Jan knew Liz had a point. She'd felt that way herself lately. But she wasn't sure Liz's church was what she needed. She'd heard some weird things about those prayer meetings. Sometimes they took you into little rooms afterwards and put their hands on your head. One friend who'd visited there had even come back to school saying they expected her to have some sort of renewal of the heart or something before they'd let her go home."

"I think our pastor was right, Jan," said Liz, still pressing it. "You have to be reborn inside. Religion won't be very exciting to you until that starts to happen."

"And you think a prayer service at City Temple would do it, right?"

"Well, it couldn't hurt."

JAN THOUGHT about the conversation the rest of the day. She didn't go to prayer meeting with Liz on Wednesday night. The conversation still churned in her, though. She wondered if her confirmation should have made a difference. Or if what she needed was something like City Temple.

Friday morning Jan did something she thought she would never do. She phoned the pastor at Trinity Church. She made an appointment to speak with him that afternoon.

When she arrived, had parked her bike outside the office, and was seated in the pastor's study, she wondered if coming had been a good idea. Pastor Strong sat down across from her and smiled. She'd slept through some of his classes during confirmation instruction. And a lot of his sermons. Now, here she was, sitting looking at him, one-on-one.

"We missed you Sunday, Jan. I hope you're feeling better. Your folks said you had a fever."

"Yeah I'm fine now." It gave her a good feeling, knowing he had at least noticed she was missing.

"What can I do for you?" asked Pastor Strong.

She wondered if he thought she was in trouble or something. Why else would a girl her age make a special appointment with the pastor in the middle of the week?

"Pastor Strong, is confirmation supposed to . . . well . . . you know . . . cause some amazing change in you or anything? I mean, I've been confirmed three months, and I don't feel any more religious than I did before."

The pastor smiled. "Good question. And good for you for asking it. A lot of kids your age just want to get religion class out of the way ao they can get on with the rest of their lives, without God if possible."

Jan nodded. She had had such thoughts a time or two.

"No. No, there isn't any miracle. The church is still the same church. The same pastor. The same people — just as sinful as we were before."

She liked the way he included himself in that last idea.

"But," Pastor Strong continued, "what can be *new* is

you. The way you think about yourself and God. It's like planting a seed, Jan. You have something growing in you. God wants it to grow. It may take months or years. But if you want it to grow strong and healthy, God's love can make you into a brand new person. It's a mystery how it happens, like the mystery in a growing plant. How can a seed turn into a tall tree? The scientists don't even know. God knows. That's how it is with you and me."

"How come some churches, like . . . you know . . . like City Temple, seem so full of life and everything?"

The pastor sighed. "I know exactly what you mean. You know, Jan, we could do that sort of thing at Trinity Church. But I think it would embarrass some of us. And others would be uncomfortable with such an emotional style. And, frankly, a lot of us would get tired of it and want something more balanced and more nourishing to the whole person."

"But how can you be sure they're wrong?"

"They're not wrong. It's just that I've seen what such a style can do to people. You see, when I was a child, my parents took me to a church exactly like that. It just didn't satisfy me as the years went by. I saw a lot of people get their hopes up in that congregation. But as time went by a lot of them were disappointed. And, after awhile, they just got tired of how the pastor scolded them for not feeling strongly enough about their faith. Now, on the other hand, our congregation seems 'old fashioned' to a lot of people. But I've found you can grow lots of brand new Christian lives in such an old, familiar garden as this church is. Just give the church a chance to help you grow, Jan. And, be sure to keep yourself open, expecting to become a new person as well."

JAN THOUGHT about the pastor's advice almost nonstop until the next Sunday morning. When she sat next to her parents in the pew, she found that the hymns, the prayers, the sermon all seemed new to her. It was the same old church. But something new was happening. And it was happening to her.

"Thanks, God," she said, praying silently. "Thanks for

giving me that fever. It got me to thinking. And to looking at things in a brand new way."

And then she vowed never to let herself get into ruts at worship. Or, in case she ever did, not to stay in them for very long.

Thought and action starters:

1. When something is almost two-thousand years old, it can get to seem a bit creaky. The liturgy of your congregation has parts that are that ancient. Before asking your pastor to throw it all out and bring in hand-clapping and guitars, however, see if you can get someone (maybe the pastor) to share some information with your youth group or Sunday class — or maybe with the congregation on Sunday morning — about why we worship as we do, and what's so good about it. If the pastor doesn't have the time, he or she will know someone who can do it.

2. There's no doubt that sometimes our worship time can get a little boring. What things could you do, personally, to make your own experience more exciting when you worship? What ideas could you share with members of the worship committee?

3. Do you think Jan's pastor handled her questions effectively? Does what he said mean people in "more emotional" congregations are inferior somehow? If not, why are there so many styles of worship in the Christian church? What can be good about all this variety?

A reading from Scripture that relates to this story is Psalm 149. Another is John 3:1-17.

Strange Parade

The least-expected things can bring a family back together. Sometimes all it takes is a faulty spark plug at church time on a summer Sunday morning.

Scott Thomason stared through the windshield of the pick-up camper, scanning the horizon for a mountain peak. This was the day they'd first be able to see the Grand Tetons. So far on this trip, all through Nebraska and Wyoming, the country had been flat, dry and boring. But on this bright summer Sunday morning that would change.

Ca-chug!

"Dad... what was that?" asked Scott, looking past his mother, who was in the middle of the seat, between him and his father.

Scott's father cursed softly, barely loud enough for Scott to hear. "It sounds — and feels — a little like the engine's trying to cut out," he said. His face displayed disgust.

Ca-chug!

"Don, I think something's wrong with it," his mother said, looking mildly alarmed.

"Those clowns at the garage back home," growled Scott's father, letting up on the accelerator. "It did the very same thing last week when I was road-testing it for this trip. They supposedly checked it over and said everything was fine. Those..."

Scott knew what was coming. When his father got disgusted, and began to get the sort of look on his face that he had right now, it meant his language would turn foul.

Scott's mother seemed to sense it too. "Don, just relax.

Look, there's a little town right up ahead. Maybe somebody can give it a look."

"On a Sunday morning? Fat chance!" Scott's father retorted.

Ca-chug!

"Well, looks like we don't have much choice," he said, slowing at the "city limits" sign.

Scott felt his heartbeat quicken. It made him uneasy when he his father lost his temper, which he seemed to do a lot.

His father pulled the pick-up into the parking area of the one station that seemed to be open. Turning off the key, he looked impatiently at his watch. "Nine-forty-five. And here we are, stuck in some podunk!" Getting out, he slammed the driver's door angrily and marched off toward the station office.

"Well," Scott's mother said, exhaling heavily, "this may turn out to be a long day. Let's just make the best of it."

Scott opened the passenger door and climbed down, waiting for his mother to get out before slamming it solidly shut.

"Let's take a walk," she said. "We can probably get a tour of the whole town in about ten minutes, from the looks of it."

"Really," Scott said, laughing. "Think we ought to tell Dad where we're going?"

"I think we should just let your father cool off," she said, nodding toward Main Street.

There was only a block of stores in the tiny business district. None seemed to be open. In the block beyond they came to a small white frame church. "Community United Church," the bulletin board said. Underneath was the announcement:

**SUMMER WORSHIP SCHEDULE:
SUNDAYS 10:00 A.M.**

A handful of adults was going in the front door. As each opened it, Scott could hear organ music floating out. "Mom, what time is it?" he asked.

"Ten minutes before ten. Why?"

"I just thought of something. Our Sunday class teacher back home said he'd give us extra credit if we brought back bulletins from churches we visited on vacation. Do you want to go to church?"

"Well . . . I don't know . . . your father . . ."

"Yeah, but who knows how long they may be tied up there at the gas station?"

"Well, we'd at least better tell him where we're going, don't you think?"

"Yeah, I guess. And if he gets done sooner, he can just come down and get us."

"More like 'wait in front for us,' I'd say." Scott's father never went to worship with the two of them.

When they got back to the gas station, Scott's father was leaning over the engine of the pick-up, watching carefully everything the mechanic did.

"Dad, Scott and I are going to church up the street. It's just a block and a half from here. Okay?"

Scott's father mumbled something, not even looking away from the engine. "Did you hear me, Don?" she asked, brushing her hand along his shoulder. He nodded, but still didn't look away.

On the way back to the church, his mother said, "What's this about getting 'extra-credit' in Sunday class. I thought all that stopped when you were confirmed."

Scott chuckled. "Yeah. Well, some of us in Mr. Leonard's class just keep on doing it. It's sort of a contest some of us have going. He says anybody with 500 points by Christmas gets free pizza, his treat. So we're pushing him."

"You've got me curious, Scott. If you weren't having the contest, would you have suggested going to church just now?"

"Huh. Oh. Sure. Wasn't that what we said we would try to do when we were confirmed? Anyway, you wanted to go, didn't you?"

"Well. Yes. And actually, Scott, I'm impressed that you suggested it. A lot of kids your age would have forgotten about church. Especially on vacation."

They walked into the tiny church building just as the bell in the tower above the entryway began to ring. As they slipped into a back pew, Scott looked around the plain worship area. There appeared to be only about two dozen people there. And no kids, as far as he could see.

The congregation started singing the first hymn. Scott realized he'd forgotten to pick up a bulletin. He studied the hymn board for the number, then found the page. "When peace like a river . . . " read the first phrase. His mom had sung that as a solo once, back in their home church. And his dad hadn't even come to church to hear it.

When the time came for the Scripture readings, a member of the congregation got up to read. Scott noticed he was wearing blue jeans, a cowboy shirt, and a rope tie with a silver slide on it.

Scott glanced about the room again. Almost everybody there was wearing casual clothes, just like the reader. He turned the pages in the Bible, then started reading:

> *The wolf shall dwell with the lamb, and the leopard shall lie down with the kid, and the calf and the lion and the fatling together . . .*

Weird, Scott thought. Tame animals and wild animals making friends with each other. Whoever wrote that had to be kidding!

Then the pastor came out to the step in front of the altar. He looked over the congregation for a minute, then said, "Peace!"

"Peace," some of the congregation answered.

"Did you mean that, friends? I did," the pastor said. "That's what I want to talk about these next few minutes. Peace. You just heard Calvin read about it in Isaiah, chapter eleven . . . "

Scott enjoyed the casual way the pastor presented his sermon, not even going into the pulpit. He just stood in front of the congregation and talked without any notes or anything.

Suddenly Scott's father slid into the pew, next to his mother. Scott was amazed. He was certain it was the first time he'd ever seen his dad in a church building.

He heard his father whisper to his mother, "They fixed it faster than I thought. Just a spark plug. I'm parked out in front. Let's go."

Just then Scott realized the members of the congregation were all turned and looking straight at him! Had his father's whispering been *that* loud?

"Now, please understand, you don't have to if you don't want to," said the pastor, looking right at Scott. "But since you're the only young person in the building today, I really would appreciate your help."

Scott looked at the pastor and gave him a bewildered "Who, me?" sort of look.

"Would you please come up here to the front and help me?" invited the pastor.

Scott felt his face turn warm. He looked quickly at his parents. They seemed as confused as he did. Before he knew what he was doing, his feet were carrying him along the side aisle, up to the front of the church.

"Thanks," said the pastor, putting his arm around Scott's shoulders. "Now, to finish out the sermon, I think we should have a 'peace parade.' Our volunteer here . . . what's your name, friend? . . . Scott? Scott, here, will begin." The pastor turned to the altar and, taking the wooden cross, its base still attached, handed it to Scott. "Since it says in Isaiah, 'A child shall lead them,' you hold this cross high over your head and lead the parade. I'll follow. Then anybody in the congregation who believes in making peace with their neighbors, we want you to join in too. We'll circle all the way around the pews a couple times and then go back to our seats."

The next thing Scott knew, he was carrying the cross down the aisle, then circling around the pews. People were getting up and joining in. The organ was playing "When peace like a river." When he got back to the front of the church the first time, Scott noticed something that made his heartbeat double. His mother was walking in the parade. And right behind her was his father! And he had a big smile on his face.

Twenty minutes later they were in the pick-up, riding

west, heading for the Grand Teton mountains.

"Say, Scott," his father said all of a sudden, "why didn't you tell me church could be that much fun? Maybe I'll come with you and Mom once in a while from now on."

Scott felt electricity race through him. It had been exciting enough, leading the strange parade around the church. But this was even more terrific.

It was not until much later that he realized he'd forgotten to ask the usher for a bulletin.

Thought and action starters:

1. Sometimes teenagers report that, after being involved in helping to plan and lead part of a worship service, they have a whole new attitude about worship. Have you had an opportunity to take a leadership part in the service? Would you like to? Would your pastor or worship planning group be open to it? How about suggesting a service planned and presented by teenagers (with advice from an adult)?

2. It's not easy keeping your confirmation promise to continue faithfully at worship when members of your own family don't participate with you. If you've been slipping lately, think about friends you have who may not be members of your family but who have been regular at worship and who could encourage you by having you attend with them. (Perhaps you could "adopt" a friend for such a purpose, possibly a classmate and his/or her family.)

3. Scott's father may have had reasons for not going to church with his wife and son. Try to imagine what some of those reasons could have been. If you had had a chance to talk to him, would you have had an idea to share with him that might have made him think again about giving up on the church?

A reading from Scripture that relates to this story is Isaiah 11:1-10.

A Real Steal

When she snagged her part-time job, Robin was the envy of all her friends. But then she started having pangs of conscience. In her situation, what would you have done?

Robin Northwood tucked still one more silk daisy into the artificial flower arrangement in the straw basket. It was her best creation yet. Only three weeks into her work at The Unique Boutique, she had become a real asset to the shop.

That, at least, was what Carol Lombardy kept on telling her. Carol owned the boutique and had offered Robin the chance to work after school week days. The salary was not the greatest, but she was only a tenth-grader, after all. And lots of kids her age could not get part-time jobs no matter where they looked.

Lifting the basket from the work table, Robin carried it with pride into the salesroom. Setting it in place beside the half-dozen others she had created in the last two days, she turned to find a tag. Jotting the price onto the scrap of card attached to the looped string, she thought, "How can this basket and these flowers be worth $4.95? Carol couldn't have paid nearly that much for them." But then she thought, "You have to make some kind of profit, after all, or you won't stay in business very long."

Carol Lombardy came breezing out of her private office. Robin admired Carol's brisk efficiency, and the elegant clothes she always wore. She made the boutique look classy, the way she dressed. She probably was forty, Robin thought, but looked like thirty. It was how she dressed, and wore her hair and makeup.

"Robin, I've got a project for you," said Carol, smoothing the sleeve of her linen blouse where it came over the elbow. "All the woven goods — the baskets, things like that — I want you to remove them from the shelves and take them back into the workroom. Then we're going to make new price tags. Mark them all up by ten dollars each."

Robin's eyes grew big as saucers. "You mean . . . you mean, if it was $4.95, I should reprice it at $14.95?"

"That's right," said Carol, her brown eyes sparkling and animated. "I just got the franchise for exclusive boutique sales in Scottwood's Terrace Mall."

Robin had heard of the ritzy shopping center by that name. She'd never been into that neighborhood. She had heard that some of the houses over there were built along little parkways with gates and checkpoints: you could not go in without permission from somebody who was living there. And people over there drove Continentals and Mercedes Benzes.

In spite of herself, Robin said, "Do you really think there's $14.95 worth of stuff in one of these arrangements?"

Carol smiled tolerantly and shook her head in mock despair. "You have a lot to learn, my young assistant," she said. Her voice was not sarcastic, but Robin felt as if she were being talked down to. Carol continued: "In this business you don't worry about what something is 'worth' in actual terms. You think about what you can make it *seem* to be worth to the customer. If someone thinks we ought to charge $8.95 for your arrangements, we'll start charging that. So far, in this part of the city, $4.95 is about what the traffic will bear. Now, when we open in Scottwood we may find that the upper crust who shop there will consider $14.95 a real steal. If they do, we'll tell them it was an introductory price and increase it to, say, $24.95."

Robin blinked. She was being paid minimum wage. She wondered how much Carol was making in this business. Evidently the sky was the limit — if you could get people to pay what you asked them to.

"Actually," said Robin, starting to carry the baskets back into the workroom, "how much *does* it cost for these silk flowers and the baskets? I'm just curious."

"Sometimes curiosity can get you into trouble," Carol said, straightening a row of porcelain figurines on a glass shelf. "In this case, let's just say you're asking me to divulge private information. I think you can understand that, Robin. Okay?" She asked the last word brightly. Robin felt sheepish and wished she had not asked in the first place.

ROBIN FELT a little bit uncomfortable, riding along with Carol in her green and silver BMW. She knew these German sports cars were expensive, but she wasn't sure how much a new one cost. Carol's still smelled new, and it rode as smooth as silk.

As they rolled into the Scottwood Terrace neighborhood, Robin felt even more uncomfortable. Carol had told her she ought to wear something "extra expensive looking" for today's grand opening of The Unique Boutique franchise in Scottwood Terrace Mall. Even so, she felt completely out of place amidst the brick palatial houses set far back behind thick lawns and ornamental trees. She noticed some of the houses had what looked to her like servants' quarters behind them, some of them built upstairs over the double or triple garages. Her own parents worked in ordinary occupations. What, she wondered, did these people do to earn a living?

When they pulled up to the Terrace Mall, Carol said, "Think and act as elegantly as you can. These people can sniff out inferiority. We want them to know we completely understand their lifestyle."

But Robin knew that she did not.

The open house went smoothly. Business was brisk and non-stop. By early afternoon they'd sold out of the baskets Robin had made up the week before. Not one of the customers seemed to bat an eyelash, paying the high prices Carol had put on the merchandise. Robin was amazed, bud didn't let on to the customers.

As they rode back to the Main Street outlet of The Unique Boutique, Carol surprised Robin by saying, "I'm impressed with your good work. You haven't been here even a month yet, and already people are commenting on the good things you've created. Of course, they don't know that you're the one who did the work, but they give raves over those floral baskets you've been making. So, I think it's only fair, Robin, that I increase your salary."

"SO, HOW'S THE NEW job going, Robin?" asked her father from his easy chair. He had the television on and was tuned in to a news program that he always watched on Sunday nights.

"Oh, it's fine, Dad," she said, turning the pages of the Sunday comics. "I'm just glad Carol doesn't make me work Sundays. This six-days-a-week stuff is enough to wear you out."

"I think you know," her father said, "that if you had to work on Sunday your mother and I would not have let you take the job."

Robin was well aware of that. She'd argued with her parents once or twice about it. But they wouldn't let her take a Sunday job — especially one that would have kept her out of church and youth class. Even when she pointed out that half the kids with whom she'd been confirmed were working on Sunday mornings now, her parents hadn't budged.

"You know, Dad," she said, folding and dropping the comics, "I can't believe how some people live. I mean, like those rich families over in Scottwood."

"Nothing but the best, right?" Robin's father said, still glued to the announcer's words.

"I'll say. I mean, what do they need with all that comfort and luxury?"

"Well, think about it. We have more than we need too. You realize, don't you, that in this country we are only about six percent of the world's population, but we consume a fourth or even a half of some of the world's resources?"

Robin thought about it. It was true. Her own family was not living high on the hog. But she had never gone hungry, like some people in their city probably did some nights. And then there were the people in poor countries.

The phone rang. Her mother called out to her father to come and speak to somebody. Robin sat looking absent-mindedly at the television screen. There was a commercial inviting people to "pamper themselves" with clothes that would "give you the feel of luxury." When the announcer came back on the screen, he said, "And now a shocking look at how one business in this country takes advantage of the poorest of the poor in Mexico." The next thing Robin knew, the picture had switched to a run-down village somewhere south of El Paso, Texas. The voice of a reporter said, "How much would you pay for a basket like this woman has so carefully woven here in this small hut?" He held up a basket that looked to Robin every bit as though it had come from The Unique Boutique. "This peasant," said the man holding the basket, "works all day making these pretty baskets because she can get — not one or two dollars apiece for them but, get this — seven cents. That's right. The buyer from El Paso, who has hired this poor woman to make baskets for him, pays her seven cents for each. And if there's just a tiny flaw in it, he'll pay her half that. Now, perhaps you think that's all that basket should be worth. But get this: that El Paso buyer sells the baskets he imports from Mexico to operators of fancy gift stores all over the United States. He gets a dollar for each basket. That's right. Over a thousand percent markup."

Robin felt her heartbeat double. The screen was now showing the poor woman, looking tired, but smiling as she looked up from the basket she was weaving.

"We asked this woman how many baskets she could make in a good day," the reporter went on. "She told us, 'Six or seven. On a very good day, maybe eight'." Robin did some quick mental arithmetic. At eight baskets a day, the woman could earn 56¢. Fifty-six cents! That was six cents a day more than the amount Carol had just raised Robin's salary per hour! And Carol was selling the baskets for . . .

Robin's head was spinning. She could not put all of it together.

When her father came back into the room, he sat down again and said, "So, Carol's giving you a raise. Not bad!"

He didn't know what to make of her troubled look.

A COUPLE DAYS LATER, at suppertime, her father

reached behind him to the shelf beside the kitchen radio. He found the leather-covered Bible with her mother's maiden name imprinted on the cover in gold letters. Robin winced. Not often, but sometimes, her dad would read a Bible section after supper. That was not so bad. But then he'd make the family talk about it. It would run things late sometimes. Like now. She was supposed to go and help Carol at The Unique Boutique tonight.

Lately, though, Robin had been thinking about whether to stay on there. Ever since the television program she had seen on Sunday, she had been thinking about the poor, tired woman in the dirty village somewhere in Mexico. It was almost as though the people who bought her baskets, and the people who sold them, were all keeping that woman and her family from making a fair living.

With one ear she heard her father reading from the Gospel of Saint Luke. It was a parable about some workers in a vineyard. They decided if they could first kill the owner's son, the vineyard would be theirs. That seemed to Robin to be a weird theory. Why should they inherit the property just because they killed one of the heirs? All it amounted to was stealing.

Then it hit her. That was what was going on at The Unique Boutique. And lots of other places, where people with more wealth than they needed took advantage of the people who could not do anything about it.

"Dad?" she said when he was finished reading.

"Hmmm?" he answered, closing the book and laying it down beside his plate.

"Would you be disappointed in me if I gave up my job after school?"

"Well . . . I don't know. Why would you do that?"

"I'm just . . . I guess my heart's just not in it any more."

"You could have trouble finding something else, you know."

"I know," she said in a near whisper. "But I've come to the conclusion money isn't everything. That's what you and Mom have always said. I'm glad you taught me that."

She excused herself and went to make a phone call to The Unique Boutique.

Thought and action starters:

1. If it's true that Americans represent about six percent of the world's population but consume a quarter to one-half of all the resources on earth, what can (should) Christians in our country try to do about it?

2. Could we justify the actions of the basket buyer from El Paso by saying that Mexican peasants don't require as much money to live on in the first place?

3. What does God have to do with your part-time job (if you have one, or if you plan to get one)? Think about what portion of what you earn ought to go into the offering plate on Sunday morning. Think about Robin's parents' argument (in this story) that no employer has the right to make a worker miss worship to earn an income. Think about the kind of work (or company) you'd be willing — or unwilling — to be involved with, so as not to violate your conscience.

A reading from Scripture that relates to this story is Micah 6:6-8. Another is Luke 20:9-18.

Halloween With a Twist

When does "good clean fun" stop being quite so good and clean? Jerry Thorp discovered the hard way what can happen when you fail to say No — and then stick to it.

Buzz and Jerry were inseparable. Since elementary school they'd hung out all the time, fooling around together, playing little league on the same team, getting in scrapes together, looking out for one another. While the two of them had earned reputations as "troublemakers" as they'd moved through upper elementary and into junior high, it was Buzz who had really gotten into trouble more than Jerry. Buzz had been to juvenile hall a half-dozen times. Jerry never had. In fact, Buzz had been warned that one more time before the judge and he would be a candidate for reform school.

As Jerry thought about the ways Buzz had talked him into one prank after another — and how Buzz had always gotten caught, while he had not — he wondered what he'd do tonight if Buzz should phone. Jerry knew Buzz would phone. Tonight was Halloween. Buzz would be itching to do something crazy. And he'd want Jerry to do it with him.

Pulling out his science book, he opened it and laid it on the desk in front of him. His folks were at some party. They would be home late. Jerry had told them he was going to do some homework, then watch television for a while. His mom had left some treats for trick-or-treaters if they would come to the door. But Jerry was too old to fool around with that stuff. And he didn't want to mess with little beggars coming to the porch. So, he had turned the porch light off,

eaten some of the candy, and retreated to his room.
    He knew he was about to fail in Science. But, try as he might, he couldn't get intrested in the subject. Or in doing homework for the class. He closed the book. The phone rang. Jerry knew before he got into the hall to pick it up it would be Buzz.
    "Hey, buddy, how about some action?"
    "I don't know, Buzz. I've got . . . homework."
    "Homework! Ha! I'll bet. Since when did you become a student-type? Look, I'll be over in a couple minutes."
    "Listen, Buzz . . . "
    The dial tone interrupted.

    "TELL YOU WHAT," said Buzz, as they hiked down the sidewalk, dodging youngsters wearing costumes and carrying bags of treats, "let's leave a message somewhere."
    "Nothing that's against the law, Buzz," Jerry said, sticking his thumbs into the pockets of his blue jeans.
    "Naaah, we'll just decorate some windows. Places where the lights are out." Saying it, he reached into the bag he had brought along and pulled out a thick bar of soap. "Like here," he said, pointing to a church building on the corner of the street. "See, nobody's around. And look at all the windows."
    "Well, I don't know," Jerry said. "I thought you meant a house or something."
    "This is better," Buzz said. "Lots more windows. Tell you what. You take this side. I'll take the other. We'll meet in the back."
    "What you going to write?" Jerry asked, taking the soap Buzz handed him.
    "Anything. Who cares? Soap washes off."
    "Yeah. Guess so," Jerry said, beginning to feel interest in the project. Down the side of the church he began to move, writing the kinds of words in soap he ordinarily would write on bathroom walls at school. When he reached the back of the building there were no more windows. Buzz was not on the other side. Jogging back to the front door of the church, Jerry saw something that stopped his blood cold. Buzz was spray painting an obscenity on the church door.

"Buzz! You idiot! You jerk! That won't come off!"

"That's the idea, lamebrain," Buzz said. "Anyway, I want the message to stay on a while. I can hardly wait to cruise along this street next Sunday morning while the people are going in and out."

"Hey!" came a sharp, loud voice from the house next door to the church. Before Jerry knew what was happening, Buzz had taken off and disappeared. Surprised and scared, Jerry whirled to follow him, trying to scoop up the can of spray paint Buzz had left. Suddenly he went down, twisting his ankle. He felt pain shooting through him. He could not get up.

"WHY DID YOU do it, son?" The pastor of the congregation Buzz had vandalized sat looking at Jerry. The ice the pastor's wife had packed around his ankle didn't seem to help much. Jerry's foot was swollen, blue and throbbing.

"I . . . I don't know. Just a prank," said Jerry miserably. He had made up his mind he wouldn't let Buzz take the rap. That would mean reform school for sure.

"It's up to you," the pastor said. "You fix it, or I call the police — and your parents."

"You mean . . . if I get the paint off, you won't squeal on me?" He knew his folks would ground him for a month if they found out about this.

"That's right. But you'll have to do it before Sunday. In fact, after school tomorrow would be best. We can't have that obscenity on our church door all week."

Jerry nodded, frowning. Why had he turned his ankle? Why had he let Buzz talk him into this? Why had he stood in for Buzz? He felt angry and trapped.

"The trouble is," the pastor said, "you're not in much condition to stand on that ankle. Tell you what: you show up after school tomorrow; I'll have what we need to paint the door. I'll help you. That old door was needing new paint anyway."

Jerry gave him a grateful look. "Thanks. Thanks a lot."

"Come on," the pastor said. "I'll give you a ride home."

"Don't tell my folks, okay?"

"I'll leave you at the curb. You tell them what you want

about the ankle."

AS THEY PAINTED, Pastor Andrews said, "You know, Jerry, that message you put on our church door last night wasn't the first one to be put on a church door on Halloween night."

Jerry wanted to say, "But I didn't do it." He knew he couldn't say that. Instead, he said, "Well, lots of vandalism goes on every Halloween I guess."

"That's not exactly what I meant," said Pastor Andrews. "The time I'm thinking of was over 400 years ago. A pastor did it to his own church door."

"Huh?" Jerry said, stopping his brush. He shifted on the stool the pastor had brought over so he could stay off his ankle.

"That's right. Martin Luther was his name. You ever hear of him?"

"I . . . yeah, maybe. I went to Sunday school when I was little. That was quite a while ago."

"Well, Martin Luther used the church door as a bulletin board. He hammered up ninety-five sentences for debate. He figured people would see them and stop and read them. It's a little like what you did, except that what Luther wrote was a little more useful."

"What exactly did he put up on his door?" asked Jerry, starting to paint once again.

"Arguments, mostly. Things designed to make people in the church stop and think. Something you should have done, I'd guess."

"Yeah. Really," Jerry said, feeling sheepish.

"The first sentence on Luther's list was the idea that our whole life should be one of repentance."

"Oh?"

"That's right. And I guess that's sort of what you're doing right now. You're really showing me you're sorry. In exchange, I'm letting you off, not telling your parents or the police."

"So what I'm doing is repentance?" Jerry said, a little surprised at the idea.

"Sure. You're sorry, aren't you?" Pastor Andrews said,

dipping his brush back into the paint.

"Yeah. Yeah, I guess I am." He really was.

"Well, anyway, one good thing came from all of this. Besides a new coat of paint for the church door."

"What?"

The fact that I met you. It sounds to me you don't have much to do with church or God these days. Or am I wrong?"

Not really. We never go. Used to a little bit."

"Well, I'm not saying you have to show up in church next Sunday morning. But I'm really glad I met you. You look to me like an intelligent young man, with lots of gifts and energy. I sort of like you. And I hope I can persuade you that some of us people in the church are not so bad. Maybe you'll give the church a chance one of these days."

"Yeah. Maybe," Jerry said. He wasn't sure. But one thing he did know: this Pastor Andrews was not a half bad person. He seemed to know how to listen to a guy. Maybe he could come around some Sunday and see how he sounded when he preached.

Just maybe.

Thought and action starters:

1. All of us have heard the warning, "Don't run with the wrong crowd." On the other hand, is there anything to be said for making friends with someone in order to try to be a good influence on somebody who needs help (but is a bad influence themselves)? Do you think Jesus' mixing with sinners helps to answer this question, or was Jesus an exception to the rule?

2. "Trick or Treat for UNICEF" offers an alternative to merely "begging for candy" on October 31. Teenagers sometimes have helped organize Halloween parties for younger kids who have first gone out to collect donations for UNICEF. If nobody is doing it in your neighborhood, you might find it an interesting and rewarding activity to get started.

3. The pastor in this story gave Jerry a second chance. The story doesn't tell us what happened afterwards in Jerry's life. Make up your own ending for him.

A reading from Scripture that relates to this story is Jeremiah 31:31-34.

A-Time in the Morning

It's not easy staying close to God. It may require some discipline — and possibly a gentle nudge from someone who's had practice.

Jeff Carruthers squirmed on the hard pew. He wasn't used to all this silence during worship. Usually the organ was playing, or the pastor was saying something, or something was happening. But for some reason, Pastor Stevenson had put a lot of silence into this Thanksgiving Eve service. It made Jeff nervous.

He opened his bulletin again. "A Quiet Time for Thanks," the line read. Pastor Stevenson had just announced that everybody was supposed to have a silent talk with God, thanking him for the things that had enriched their lives. It seemed to Jeff that it had now been about half an hour since the pastor had announced that. But a quick look at his watch reminded him that it was only two and a half minutes. Still, that was a long, long time for nothing to be happening.

He shut his eyes again. Why couldn't he think of anything to be thankful for? Try as he might, all he could think of was what he was *not* too thankful for just now. For one thing, there were television programs he was missing — specials, in fact — because his folks had made him come to this service when he would have just as soon stayed home.

And for another thing, he and his dad would not be going hunting in the north woods as he had promised they would be this long weekend. Something had come up and Jeff was going to be stuck at home after all.

At last Pastor Stevenson interrupted the long silence.

"For these blessings, Lord, we thank you," he said. His head was bowed as he stood behind the altar, turned toward the congregation. Jeff felt guilty. He had not thanked God for anything.

As the organ started introducing the last hymn, Jeff realized one of his problems with praying was that he didn't do a lot of it. He didn't really know exactly what to say to God. Sometimes he wondered if God even liked the prayers Jeff prayed. It seemed to him the pastor was the expert at that sort of thing. Ordinary people couldn't be expected to do it quite as well, could they?

"Now thank we all our God," the congregation started singing. Jeff's mind turned to turkey dinner with the relatives tomorrow. And the football games they'd all be watching when his aunt and uncle came. For those things he felt some thanks. "He realized he probably should have thanked God for them.

He stopped singing, closed his eyes, and quickly said, "Thanks for all the good stuff we'll be having at our house tomorrow, God. Amen."

"HEY, MOM, where'd you get this basket full of groceries?" Jeff asked as his mother opened the car trunk. The basket was decorated with ribbon and was loaded with canned goods and fruit.

"The women's group is taking one of these to every shut-in on our list. And by the way, Jeff, I need you to run this basket over to old Mrs. Graham in the morning. Can you do that for me?"

"Awwwww, ma," Jeff whined. "I don't even know old lady Graham."

"Listen, young man," she said sternly, "in the first place, that's no way to talk about a woman like sweet Hilda Graham. And in the second place, I have Thanksgiving Dinner to get ready. Unless *you* would like to do the cooking for the relatives tomorrow."

Jeff felt trapped. Why was his mother always volunteering him to do errands he hadn't asked for? But he knew there wasn't any point complaining about it. He'd have to do it whether he liked it or not.

MRS. GRAHAM'S LIVING ROOM was full of old, old furniture. Jeff sat in the saggy chair beside the table with the dusty-looking doily and waited for Mrs. Graham to come back with cookies and a glass of milk. Jeff felt like a real jerk, letting this white-haired old woman, whom he didn't even know, convince him to sit down and eat a snack. He felt a little guilty too. From the looks of things, old Mrs. Graham could hardly walk. His mom had told him she had arthritis so bad she hardly could get up from the couch once she had sat down. He figured it must give her an awful lot of pain. She used a metal walker to get through the doorway of the living room and into her small kitchen. He wondered how she would ever make it back again, carrying cookies and a glass of milk.

Somehow old Mrs. Graham managed it. She had insisted Jeff sit down and let her bring the snack. Now he held his breath, watching how she shuffled, balancing the tray on the walker. Boy, he thought, she sure was stubborn, putting herself through such agony and trouble just to prove she could do it without assistance.

When she had sat down and Jeff was chewing on a cookie, she said, "We have so much to be thankful for . . . "

Jeff almost choked on the cookie. How could she say that? She was almost completely crippled. From the looks of things, she didn't have much money either. And her eyesight wasn't very good. How could she possibly be thankful for a life like that?

"Did you give God thanks today?" she asked in a kind voice.

Jeff blinked. "I . . . no, I guess I didn't."

"Well, why ever not?" she asked, still using her kind voice. "This is Thanksgiving Day, you know."

"I know," said Jeff. "We . . . probably will give thanks when we have our meal."

"Oh, certainly you will," she said. "But you don't want to wait until the middle of the day to talk to God, do you?"

Jeff looked at her. What did she mean?

"The way I see it." Mrs. Graham said, "we need to save our best time to give thanks to God. That's what I call my A-time."

" 'A-Time'?"

"That's right. A-time. I discovered, way back when I was a little girl, that if I didn't save the best part of my day to talk to God, I never talked to God at all. So one day I divided up my time. My morning time I called my A-time. That was time when I was wide awake and full of energy. I always tried to save some of that time to talk to God. Then there was B-time. That was when I was busier and might not have a chance to give God all the quiet, thoughtful time I thought I should. And C-time was leftover time. I might be doing busy work, or running errands, or other things that kept me from taking time to talk to God. And of course D-time is the worst. That was the time like just before going to sleep. Now I know some people say their prayers just then. In my case, I always found myself drifting off just then. I didn't think God appreciated me falling asleep right in the middle of a conversation with him. So I decided always to talk to God during A-time. And for me, A-time is in the morning."

Jeff felt embarrassed. He had never thought much about talking to God, regardless what time it was.

"When is your A-time?" Mrs. Graham asked, smiling at Jeff.

"I . . . guess I don't exactly know."

"Well, maybe you should think about it. Your A-time might not be the same time of day that mine is. But the main thing is, remember to save your best time to talk to God. And, don't forget to thank him for the many, many good things he keeps doing for us day by day."

He looked at Mrs. Graham's silver walker and felt guiltier than ever.

IT WAS NOT until the following Monday morning, on the school bus, riding toward Lincoln Junior High, that Jeff thought again about the visit he had had with Mrs. Graham. Suddenly he realized he still did not know when his A-time was. As he considered it, he came to the conclusion that his A-time could be time when he was riding on the bus. He didn't have to do much just at those times except sit and think anyway. It would be a good time to have a conversation with God, and to thank him for the new day, and all the good things in his life.

Looking out the bus window, at the light poles and the houses and the intersections as they all flew by, Jeff said silently, "Hello, Lord. I guess I haven't bothered to talk much to you for quite a while. Well, this is your friend, Jeff Carruthers. And I just want to tell you, I'm looking forward to today. So thanks for giving it to me. And thanks for everything that makes my life so good. Especially gym class. And my folks. And for protecting me last night while I was sleeping."

It was amazing how many things he was suddenly able to think of to be thankful for. Last week in church he couldn't think of much of anything.

His eye caught sight of an old woman walking with a cane. She stepped down from the curb with difficulty. Jeff thought a moment, and then added, "And, Lord, thanks . . . especially thanks . . . for Mrs. Graham."

Thought and action starters:

1. Mrs. Graham's question is a good one for each one of us: "When is your A-time." Think about it. Then, if you have not already done so, block out some time during this period each day and build a prayer life. Keep it conversational.

2. Is it possible to be blinded by so much "stuff" in life that we can't see what we have to be thankful for? Why do you suppose it is that the more wealth people accumulate, the smaller the proportion of income usually becomes which ends up in the offering plate?

3. Make a list of the ten things you're most thankful for. Write them down and try putting dollar values on them (if your list is carefully made, you will have some items too valuable for a price tag). Where in your list does God's promised love and faithfulness rank?

A reading from Scripture that relates to this story is Psalm 136.

Christmas in Reverse

What would happen if you asked your friends and family not to give you anything for Christmas? Try it sometime. You might be surprised.

"Pass the macaroni and cheese — and don't take any," fourteen-year-old Tom said to his brother. Twelve-year-old Jake made a face at his older brother and pushed the casserole dish toward him. Neither noticed their mother scowling at them as she watched the episode.

Tom heard the heavy sigh she let escape, however. "Watzamatta, Ma?" he said, slurring out the question with an easy grin on his face.

"Oh, I don't know," she said, sighing again. "I just wish you two would treat each other with a little more respect."

"You mean the way you and Dad used to treat each other?" Tom was sorry that he said it as soon as the words were out. Dad had moved out over a year ago. There was hardly enough money to pay the bills since then. "Sorry, Mom," he said, not grinning this time.

Mom sighed a third time. "Listen, you two," she said, trying to sound stern, "I guess you know there isn't going to be much of a Christmas around here this year. I've decided each of you will have to make a list of things you want the most. You can count on getting one thing this time. And if everything on your list is too expensive, I'll pick something myself. Got that?"

Tom and Jake stared at each other. "Cripes, what a gyp!" said Jake, kicking Tom accidentally underneath the table.

"You jerk!" Tom snapped. He returned the kick. Jake

yelped, backing suddenly away from the table. He formed an ugly retort with his mouth, but didn't say it.

"Or maybe we should just cancel Christmas," Mom said, staring angrily from one son to the other. "Tom, get that devotional book we haven't used for a while. Tomorrow's Sunday. Let's read something out of it."

"Aw, Ma, I'm going to miss my TV program."

"Well, then read a prayer at least. I think the last one in the book is for the Advent season. Try that one."

"How come he always gets to read?" Jake whined.

"Here, crybaby, you read it," Tom said, tossing the booklet at his brother. Almost at wits end, Mom didn't react to the last exchange.

Jake read the prayer for Advent. His brother looked bored, but listened anyway. By the time Jake had said the "Amen," Tom found himself thinking about the words. He was the last one to get up and leave the table.

THE NEXT DAY in church the pastor preached about "Preparing the way for the Coming of the King." He told the congregation they could best prepare for Jesus' coming by helping the poor and hungry have a better life. Since Jesus came caring for people like that, said the pastor, we should do the same.

On the way home Tom wondered if his family was part of the "poor and hungry" the pastor was talking about, now that Dad was gone and not sending much money to help out. As Mom drove along the street toward their house, Tom glanced at the back cover of the Sunday worship folder. "Your gift can help build a garden tractor for a hungry farm family in South America," the picture story said.

"Oh, by the way you two," Mom said, as she pulled into the garage, "I need those Christmas lists from both of you today. There isn't much time left to do the shopping. And, don't forget: just one thing from your list. You might as well number them — first choice, second, and so forth."

THAT EVENING Tom walked into Jake's room without knocking. "Get out of here, creep!" snarled Jake, leaning over the paper he'd been working on at his desk.

"Take your smell back to your own room."

"Just cool it a minute," Tom said, sitting down on Jake's bed. "I got something that I need to talk to you about."

"Yeah? What?" asked Jake, sounding skeptical.

"Well, look. I've been working on this Christmas list."

"So?"

"So I'm having trouble finishing it."

"You kidding? I've got ten things on my list already."

"Yeah. I have a lot of things I can put down. But I just can't give this to Mom."

"Why not? You get so greedy everything's more expensive than she can afford?"

Tom frowned and looked as though he was thinking of an insult to hurl at his brother. Instead he said, "You remember that prayer you read at supper last night?"

"No," said Jake honestly.

"Well, I've been thinking about it. In fact, I have the book right here. Listen to this." He opened the devotional book and began to read from the Advent prayer they'd shared at supper the night before: "Keep us from turning Advent into Christmas and Christmas into an unnecessary time of greedy emptiness."

"Oh, I remember something from that prayer," Jake said suddenly. "It said there's too many blue-light specials. That was kind of a weird thing to have in a prayer. Remember?"

"Yeah. And this was in there too: '... too many gifts to buy for people who may not need gifts at all'."

Jake looked carefully at Tom, waiting to hear what he'd say next.

"So, I got to thinking. Mom is running short of money. She's tired most of the time these days. She'd have to go out and buy us stuff. And, let's face it, you and I already have a bunch of stuff. We don't really need anything right now. Anyway, we're not starving or anything."

"So what? Nobody else is starving either."

"Oh yeah? Just look at this." Tom shoved the wrinkled bulletin he'd saved from church toward his brother. "Look at this skinny farmer in South America. If he had a decent tractor, he could start to feed himself, and his hungry family.

If enough people like us, who aren't hungry, gave some money for a tractor, people like him wouldn't have to worry all the time."

Jake looked at the picture, then at his brother. "You mean . . . you think we should . . . you don't want anything for Christmas?"

"Look, Jake, we already got our Christmas present. Jesus came, right? He's already here. That's the best present in the world."

Jake wrinkled his nose. Tom thought sure he'd make some smart crack, but he didn't.

"So," Tom went on, "why do we have to buy stuff to give to each other? Remember how the pastor said in church this morning that we could prepare the way for Jesus by helping somebody in trouble?"

"I never listen to the sermons," Jake said.

"Well, I did this time," Tom replied. "And all this stuff just started to fit together."

"So, what are you saying we should do?"

"I think we ought to . . ." Tom stopped short. He gave his brother a strange look.

"We ought to what?" demanded Jake.

"I have a feeling you're going to laugh at me if I say this."

"Heck, no. Say it. Even if it's stupid, I won't laugh."

"You sure?"

"I'm sure. So hurry up and say it."

"Well . . . I think we ought to tell Mom not to give us anything for Christmas. We can take the money that we saved by not buying each other presents, and have her take the money she would have spent on us, and let's give it to help get one of those farm tractors."

Tom was sure Jake would think the whole idea was ridiculous. He waited for him to say so. Instead, Jake said, "Instead of *getting* presents, we'd be *giving* one. That's sort of like Christmas in reverse, isn't it."

"Yeah. Yeah, I guess it sort of is," Tom said, sounding relieved. "What do you think? Is it worth trying?"

Jake screwed up his face into a thoughtful scowl. Then he shrugged and said, "Heck. Why not. Let's try it. Maybe for once in your life you've got a good idea."

In spite of himself, Tom gave his brother a broad grin.

Thought and action starters:

1. Brothers and sisters can be a real pain sometimes. What secrets have you discovered to getting along successfully with them while you all still live in the same house?

2. What would happen in your family if you tried to celebrate the festival of Christmas for one year the way Tom and Jake decided to do it? Who in your family do you think would have the greatest difficulty getting used to it?

3. Try to get a copy of the Alternative Celebrations Catalog (Pilgrim Press). For free information on new and creative ways to celebrate a lot of things, write to Alternatives, P.O. Box 1707, Forest Park, Georgia 30051.

4. Write to Self Help, Inc., Waverly, Iowa 50677 for information about how you and your family or friends can help to send a simple tractor to a farmer in a developing country.

A reading from Scripture that relates to this story is Luke 2:1-21. Another is Matthew 25:31-46.